MUMMY

Book # 5 in the TIME SOLDIERS® Series

Written by
KATHLEEN DUEY

Directed & Photographed by
ROBERT GOULD

Digital Illustrations & 3D Special Effects by
EUGENE EPSTEIN

One rainy morning, six neighborhood kids find a time portal in the woods. Through a swirling green light, they can see a living dinosaur! They can't convince their parents the portal exists—but it's *very* real. They pack their camping gear and go through it, armed with a video camera. They outrun and outwit a T-Rex and make it home with an incredible videotape. But before they can show it to anyone, a mysterious man wearing a dark suit steals it.

The portal opens again the very next day. Then nearly a year goes by before it opens a third time, leading them into a pirate battle. The next adventure takes the Time Soldiers to medieval England.

Dinosaurs, pirates, knights, kings: with every adventure the Time Soldiers learn what to take with them and how to survive. But they still can't figure out what makes the time portal open or why the four oldest Time Soldiers—Jon, Adam, Rob, and Mariah—can't go through it anymore. They have found new Time Soldiers to replace the older kids. The newest member is Luke. While they wait for the time portal to open again, all of the Time Soldiers exercise, study history, and learn survival skills. Caitlyn is even more impatient than the others. Her family is moving at the end of the summer—this is her last chance to be part of another amazing adventure.

On a sunny Saturday morning, Mikey finally saw the swirling green light in the woods again. The Time Soldiers got ready quickly. They ran into the time portal and a few seconds later, they were standing on a smooth, dusty stone floor in the dark. The air was still and there was a strange, sharp smell. Caitlyn flipped on her flashlight.

"This is incredible," Luke whispered. "Are we in an Egyptian pharaoh's tomb?"

Caitlyn nodded. "We're inside a pyramid. And if I only get to have one more adventure with you guys, I'm glad it's this one. The Valley of the Kings!" She grinned.

"I wish you weren't moving," Mikey said.

"We have to get a camera," Bernardo said. Their video camera was at the bottom of a river in medieval England. They were saving up for a new one.

Brian walked closer to the open sarcophagus and caught his breath. The mummy was lying inside it. The heavy lid had been moved—but the tomb hadn't been robbed.

How long had the mummy been here? He ran his hand over the carved sarcophagus. A hundred years? A thousand? He felt something loose beneath his fingers—it was an amulet set into a niche in the stone. He turned to show the others and saw Caitlyn walking toward him.

"A real mummy," she whispered, standing beside him. "It's so creepy to think that there is a preserved person under all that old cloth…"

A rustling sound made them both jump back and Caitlyn cried out. Brian slid the amulet into his pocket. Had the mummy *moved?* He could feel his heart pounding.

"We heard something," Caitlyn told the others.
Luke cleared his throat nervously. "Let's get out
of here."
No one argued.

Mikey led the way into a narrow gap between the huge stones. Their footsteps seemed very loud in the complete silence of the pyramid. Caitlyn shivered, even though it wasn't cold.

"We have to be careful," Mikey said, slowing down, "These passages were designed to be confusing."

"We're inside a 3-D maze," Bernardo reminded them.

"We have to stay oriented or we could get lost in here."

Caitlyn got out her compass. "I'll keep track of direction changes."

Bernardo nodded. "I'll memorize the turns we take." He led the way. There were steep ledges and twisting passageways.

They had to belly-crawl through one low-ceilinged tunnel. Scrambling out, they found themselves in a big chamber with a high ceiling—and no doors. Silently, they all turned to look back toward the low passageway. It was the only way out.

Brian aimed his flashlight at the paintings on the wall. They showed a boy with long black hair, then

a teenager, and then a tall man—it was the story of an entire life. Brian stared at the beautiful paintings. Then he remembered the amulet. He was angry with himself—and embarrassed. He hadn't meant to take it. The noise had startled him and they had all gotten scared, and he had forgotten it was in his pocket.

He showed the amulet to everyone and explained how he had found it. "Should I leave it here? We might not find our way back to the burial chamber."

No one knew what to say.

"Let's just get going," Luke said. "I just want to

"What if there isn't one?" Caitlyn asked quietly. They all looked at her. "The books we read all said that the pyramids were built to keep robbers out ...or trapped inside forever!"

"The portal will open inside the pyramid when it's time to go home," Mikey reminded them.

"This place gives me the creeps," Luke said quietly. Brian held the amulet tightly. "I just wish we had gone a little further back in time. If we had, this pyramid wouldn't have been finished yet and we could have gotten out." He turned to look toward the painted walls again and blinked. "Is that the time portal opening?" The amulet was suddenly

so hot against his skin that he nearly dropped it. Startled, he shoved it into his pocket and felt it burning against his leg.

"It is!" Caitlyn breathed. "The portal is opening!"

"Let's go," Bernardo said as he led the way into the light.

When Brian stepped out of the portal, he stared, amazed. They were back in the burial chamber, but now the sarcophagus was empty. The clothes, furniture, and everything else the Egyptians thought their pharaoh would need in the afterlife was there—but it was all brand new.

"This is exactly what I wished for," Brian said slowly,

He pulled out the amulet and described how the stone had gotten hot. "We went further back in time." He passed the amulet around—it was cool now.

Mikey grinned. "Does this mean we can make the portal open anywhere?"

Brian slid the amulet into his pocket. "I hope so."

Bernardo shrugged. "Or maybe the portal hiccupped."

The Time Soldiers decided to borrow clothes from the burial chamber so that anyone who saw them from a distance wouldn't notice them. The cloth was smooth and soft, and everyone found something that fit. They hid their big packs and helmets and carried only their small belt-packs, filled with bare necessities and a few surprises for emergencies.

Brian found a linen bag and decided to use it instead.
"Everyone ready?" Mikey asked.

"Incredible!" Caitlyn whispered as they came out on a ledge. "They're building the Sphinx. This *is* the Valley of the Kings!"

Bernardo was grinning. "I've been hoping we'd get to see the pyramids."

"There are probably mummies in all of them," Mikey said quietly, looking down the valley.

Luke nodded. "This whole valley is a giant
graveyard for ancient kings and queens. Amazing."
Everyone fell silent, staring.
Mikey sighed. "I wish we had a camera."

Caitlyn was so excited she felt breathless. "The pyramids are huge," she said. "They have to start building them when the person is born in order to finish in time for his burial."

They were all quiet, thinking about everything they had studied. Making a person's body into a mummy

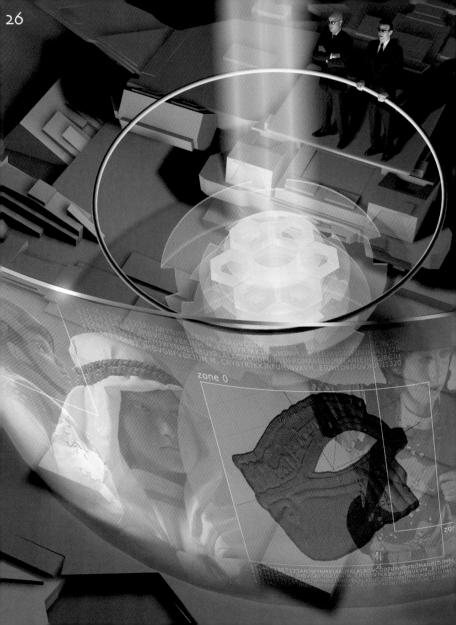

the Egyptian board game on the Internet as part of their research. Brian frowned and glanced up. "Now he's saying it'll be interesting to see if Mikey's pale skin will get darker and if his light colored eyes will turn brown as we get older."

Mikey frowned. "It's like he thinks of us as his pets or something."

The boat floated past cornfields and groves of date palms. Mikey spotted a temple and pointed it out to the others. They all stayed very still, staring. Seeing ancient Egypt was a dream come true.

"The sky is so blue," Bernardo said. "It's like this every time we come through the portal."

"No pollution," Mikey said. "There are no cars yet."

"Can they understand us when we're holding the amulet?" Luke asked.

Brian called out to the pharaoh. "Where are you taking us?" The boy king's face was blank. It was clear he hadn't understood.

Brian whispered what the Egyptians were saying so everyone would know. The pharaoh and his sister argued about the senet game and the pharaoh finally grabbed the game board and threw it into the river. One of the guards laughed softly. The pharaoh glanced at him and the man bowed low to apologize.

"And the walls are made of painted mud bricks, remember?" Caitlyn whispered. "That's why none of the palaces are still standing in our time. Only the pyramids, the temples, and the statues were made of stone."

Once they were inside the palace, the pharaoh
spoke to the guards again.

"We're going to a party," Brian translated. "He
told them to get us ready so he can show us to
his relatives and friends."

A moment later, the pharaoh and his sister
disappeared through a wide doorway. The guards

closed in again and walked quickly, hurrying the Time Soldiers along. They were all nervous, glancing around as they went, trying to memorize passage-ways in case they got a chance to escape. One thing was obvious—the pharaoh was used to getting his own way, every time. He was powerful, and he was dangerous.

The guards herded the Time Soldiers into a small room, then closed the door. There was very little light and the only window was set high in the wall.

"We're trapped," Mikey said.

Brian held the amulet tightly. "I could try to make the portal open to take us home."

"Not yet," Caitlyn said. "Please!"

In the dim light, Brian could see Luke nodding. Bernardo smiled. "I don't want to leave yet, either. It's too amazing to see all this and the pharaoh doesn't seem to want to hurt us."

They took a vote. None of them wanted to leave. Not yet.

A servant came and handed each of them a little cone-shaped piece of scented wax. It was soft in the warm evening air. When they stood still, unsure what to do, the servant took the waxen cone he had given Caitlyn and pushed it into her hair. "We read about this," she whispered. "Remember? They must be taking us to a banquet or something."

The men in dark suits were smiling. "You know, once we get our hands on that stone, we could just—" one began.

"Don't even say it," his companion interrupted.

The first man sighed and then he nodded.

The spice-scented wax melted into their hair as they ate. After the banquet, the pharaoh challenged them to a game of senet. "If one of us can beat him," Brian translated, "he'll let us go. If not...we'll be his servants for the rest of our lives."

"Bernardo, you beat the rest of us at senet when we were researching ancient Egypt," Mikey whispered

Bernardo thought about it. "I wish I had practiced more."

"Concentrate on every move," Mikey said. "Take your time."

The Pharaoh's servants brought his chair and made him comfortable. Then the game began.

Bernardo played well and he was lucky—he got three of his markers in a row to block the pharaoh. On the last throw Bernardo moved all his game tokens off the board.

"I won," he said, grinning. "I can't believe I beat him!"

The pharaoh gave an order in a voice so low that Brian couldn't hear. An instant later, guards came. "Stay calm," Mikey said. But it was hard—the pharaoh looked furious and they were all scared that he wouldn't keep his word.

The guards pushed the Time Soldiers back down the passageway to the little room they had been in before.

"The pharaoh won't keep his word. We have to escape," Bernardo whispered as the guards closed the door behind them.

They all tried to find a way out. They stood on

each other's shoulders to reach the window, but it was too high. Then they heard voices in the corridor. Someone was talking to the guard. They crowded around the door.

Brian squinted through the crack between the door and the wall. "It's that servant who kept hanging around our banquet table. He's bribing the guard!"

They all jumped back as the door opened.

"Give me the amulet," the servant hissed. "I know you have it." He lunged at Brian, grabbing his wrist.

He forced Brian's hand open and wrenched the amulet free, then whirled and ran, pounding down the corridor. Before the startled guard could react, the Time Soldiers chased the thief down the long hallway.

The men in dark suits were staring at their monitors.
"Did he get the stone?" one of them demanded.
His companion shrugged. "From the way the kids
are reacting..."
"No!" the first man groaned as their monitors
flickered, then went dark. "They'll never get it back."
He pounded his fist on the console. "I can't believe

we got this close…and now the stone is lost to some common thief?"

The second man shrugged. "He looked familiar."

The first man looked up sharply. "What?"

The second man was frowning. "You heard me."

The man sprinted up the corridor, then leaped out a low, arched opening in the wall.

"Follow him!" Brian whispered hoarsely.

The man stumbled as he landed and the Time Soldiers were able to see which way he ran. They followed, the angry shouts from the palace fading as they rounded a corner.

Bernardo saw a few people turning to watch as they raced past, but it was getting too dark for anyone to get a good look at them. They kept running as the moon rose, chasing the thief, the dry dust muffling their footfalls.

Finally, they came to the outskirts of the city, passing the last of the houses. They had all kept up pretty easily—and the thief was slowing down. They could see him in the moonlight and it was clear he was getting tired.

"Drop back," Mikey said, quietly. "Let him think he lost us."

Date palms and pomegranate orchards lined the road as they kept going. They stayed hidden, following the man who had taken the amulet

The exhausted thief dropped back to a walk, then stopped, turning to look. The Time Soldiers hid. After a long moment, the man started walking again.

"Is that a temple?" Brian whispered, pointing.

A little breeze stirred the leaves. Somewhere a rooster woke and crowed at the moon. The Time Soldiers followed cautiously, quietly.

The temple guards called out and the man answered.
Then he staggered and fell. "He told them he's sick,"
Brian whispered. Then he crept closer to watch. The
man was faking illness, but he was really burying
something in the sand. The amulet? When the man
finally staggered away, Brian went back and told
the others what he had seen.

"He's clever," Caitlyn said. "The guards left him alone because the sick were allowed to pray at the temples."

"We'll never get the amulet back," Luke said sadly. "We can't pass as Egyptians and if the guards catch us, they'll probably take us to the pharaoh."

"Do you think the servant is just a thief—or does he know about the amulet somehow?" Caitlyn asked. No one answered. No one knew what to say. They could hear the night breeze rustling the palm fronds.

"We have to get it back," Brian said. "And I have a plan." He handed Luke a long, slim box he had saved from the Fourth of July. Luke's eyes widened

Mikey nodded. "It ought to work."
"We'll stay close," Bernardo promised. "Be careful."

While the others got ready, Brian watched the guards. The instant he saw them turn to stare, he ran, staying low, then dropped to his knees to dig frantically. When his hands touched smooth leather, he pulled a little pouch from the sand and opened it to make sure. The amulet was inside!

"Now what?" Bernardo asked.

Mikey gestured. "We need to find a boat and get back to the pyramid. That's where the portal will reopen."

"If it doesn't," Luke said, "Brian can try wishing again." He started walking and the others followed

It took a long time, but they finally found a small
papyrus boat. They slid it into the water and started
downstream. There were two oars and they took
turns rowing, careful to stay as far from the hippos
as they could. They drank clear, cool river water
and slept in shifts, the rowers keeping watch. When
the moon was low in the sky, they heard voices on

then pointed. "There's a good place to land the boat. See the bushes growing down over the bank?" Bernardo and Luke paddled harder as Mikey steered the boat toward the shallows. "Hurry!" Bernardo said as they scrambled ashore.

With the amulet in his hand again, Brian could understand the guards as they screamed orders at the rowers. He could understand the higher-pitched shouts of the pharaoh, too. The boy was frantic to catch them.

"He's furious with the guards," Brian managed to tell the others as they ran. "He says they let us get away."

Mikey glanced back at the pharaoh's boat. The men were looking for a place with deep water near the bank so they wouldn't run aground.

"Look!" Brian shouted. "I think I see the light from the portal."

The glow from the open portal was pouring into the night. Caitlyn pulled out her compass and they started downward toward the burial chamber.

"The guards are refusing to come into the pyramid," Brian told them all, translating the shouts they could hear behind them. "They're scared of the green light."

Wish for the portal to take us home."
Brian opened the pouch, his hands trembling.
What if it didn't work? Would they be trapped
here forever with the pharaoh's mummy? Brian
held the amulet tightly and tried to concentrate.

The men in dark suits were watching closely. "What do you think?" one of them asked his companion. "Are there more pieces of the stone in the tomb?"

"Let's look," the other man said, adjusting the visual. "It shows up as deep red at this end of the wave spectrum. See anything?"

The first man shook his head. "No. But we know they have it—we can see *them*."

"And look," the second man said. "They've summoned the portal again. They're using the pomoja stone."

"Remember the men in the dark suits who stole our first videotape?" Mikey asked.

Bernardo frowned. "I've always wondered why they didn't follow us through the portal."

"They're grown-ups," Caitlyn said. "They'd probably get headaches like Jon and Mariah and Adam, or even worse, right?"

Everyone nodded. It made sense.

Brian rubbed the amulet as he listened. A patch of the black enamel lifted.

"It's glowing–like the stone the pirate had," Caitlyn whispered.

Bernardo stared. "And that weird globe in the dragon's lair."

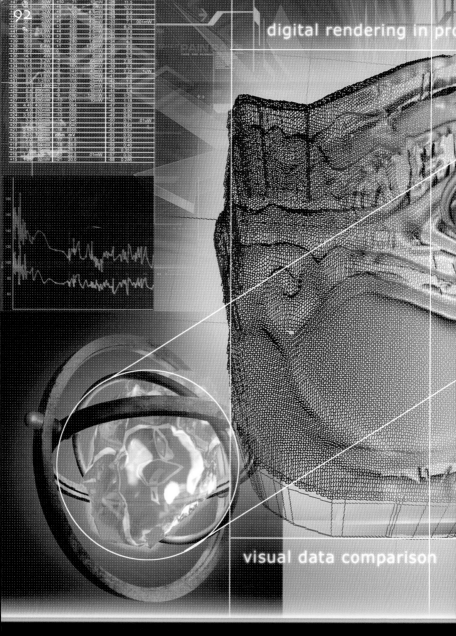

digital rendering in pro

visual data comparison

"We need every fragment of the stone we can find," one of the men said. "This makes three—"

"No," his companion interrupted. "Two. The thief looked familiar because he's the pirate from the second journey—the one who had a piece of the stone."

The first man frowned. "And he used it to open the portal and ended up in ancient Egypt? It's a wonder

probably when. But first, we have to figure out a safe place to hide the amulet."

"You all have to keep in touch," Caitlyn said sadly. "I want to know what happens."

"We'll tell you everything," Mikey promised. "If we can control the portal, the adventures are going to get even more amazing."

To be continued...

Reading is more fun with
BIGGUY BOOKS Inc ®

www.bigguybooks.com